D1550763

THE
BOOK
OF
DARES

100 WAYS FOR BOYS TO BE KIND, BOLD, AND BRAVE

RANDOM HOUSE 🏠 NEW YORK

THE
BOOK
OF
DARES

TED BUNCH & ANNA MARIE JOHNSON TEAGUE

with A CALL TO MEN

Text copyright © 2021 by A Call to Men
Cover art copyright © 2021 by Jay Roeder

All rights reserved. Published in the United States
by Random House Children's Books, a division
of Penguin Random House LLC, New York.

Random House and the colophon are registered trademarks
of Penguin Random House LLC.

Visit us on the Web! rhcbooks.com

Educators and librarians, for a variety of teaching tools,
visit us at RHTeachersLibrarians.com

Library of Congress Cataloging-in-Publication Data
is available upon request.
ISBN 978-0-593-30298-9 (hc)—ISBN 978-0-593-30299-6 (lib. bdg.)—
ISBN 978-0-593-30300-9 (ebook)

The text of this book is set in 11-point Neutraface.
Interior design by Jen Valero

Printed in the United States of America
10 9 8 7 6 5 4 3 2
First Edition

⋙ CONTENTS ⋘

Dear Boys,

The book you hold in your hands is magical. It will give you powers.

Well, okay, it won't teach you spells that can get you out of an upcoming test or that let you turn yourself into a hologram. . . . But it can help you here and now to show you the greatest trick of all: how to break out of the Man Box.

We've coined the term Man Box to describe the rules that our society expects boys to obey as they grow up and become "real men." You've probably heard people say things like "Man up!" and "Boys don't cry" and "Don't act like a girl!" These phrases are not only dangerous but insulting to the complexities of being a boy.

These messages tell you that it's not okay to show emotions or be anything less than brave, strong, and confident all the time. But boys are human! It's not just okay to be vulnerable, scared, and sad—it's natural. And yet, the Man Box isn't about that. The Man Box stops you from being your true, authentic self by limiting what you think you can do. And that isn't cool.

Just as Houdini escaped from the belly of a whale, you can escape the Man Box. But unlike Houdini, you don't need to break free in under fifteen minutes—there's no time limit here.

The Book of Dares is ongoing. You don't have to read it

from cover to cover in your first sitting, or even in your second. You can pick it up over and over, whenever you want. And you definitely don't have to do the dares in order—you can skip around to whichever ones sound most fun. The more dares you do, the more confident you'll feel about who you truly are, what makes you special, and how to treat people around you with kindness and respect. It contains all the ingredients you need to make your real life the best life.

We've spoken with thousands of boys like you around the world about the idea of dares. Unanimously, boys agree that dares are terrifying. It's impossible to know the outcome of a dare—and scary to imagine a bad one. With every dare, there's potential for embarrassment, shame, and being laughed at—in other words: judgment. There's pressure, not only to go through with the dare, but to accept the challenge in the first place. Both are ways of showing you're tough or proving your manhood.

And yet boys told us that they still find dares appealing, that they're fascinated with dare culture and the respect earned by completing dares. Not to mention that it feels a little bit like living on the edge.

Think about the last time you were dared to do something. How did it feel before and after? Were you afraid? Did it feel risky?

The dares in this book might feel risky, too, but they're based on education from more than twenty years of experience we've had working with boys in middle and high schools—as well as men in the National Football League, the National Basketball Association, Major League Baseball, Major League Soccer, the National Hockey League, the United States military, corporations, organizations, world leaders, and students in colleges and universities.

There are so many good things about being a boy—more than we can mention—and you should be able to name them if someone asks you to. A boy's strength isn't measured by his muscles or the outdated ideas that his dad's and grandad's generations followed. Strength and masculinity can be conveyed in countless ways—intelligence, vulnerability, sensitivity, empathy, the bravery to ask for help and to seek forgiveness and to challenge problematic notions.

The dares in this book will allow you to understand what healthy manhood, authenticity, leadership, and gender equity are all about. Together, the dares presented here will give you the tools to develop healthy attitudes and behaviors that value yourself and others.

Remember: you're already a great kid, and we're just here to support you in becoming the greatest version of yourself. Thank you for daring to live and grow into a healthy manhood! (And, yes, you can absolutely count that as one dare you've already successfully completed.)

—Ted and Anna Marie

DARE TO
DO SOMETHING YOU
LOVE EVEN IF IT'S NOT
SOMETHING BOYS ARE
"SUPPOSED TO DO"

ONCE YOU STOP ATTACHING GENDER TO ACTIVITIES AND OBJECTS, a world of possibilities opens up to you. Want to plant a garden? See a musical? Write a poem? Go for it! Are you afraid that the guys would give you side eye and make fun of you if they knew you wanted to do these things? Show them that men everywhere grow food and flowers in gardens, especially chefs and cooks. Show them that men go to the theater *and* perform onstage. Show them that poetry is created by men like hip-hop artist Chance the Rapper and author Robert Frost, who wrote "The Road Not Taken." Be like Frost and try a different path. Because that's being real. And being real means doing the things you love even if other people don't understand why you love them. Shutting down parts of yourself because you're afraid of how others might perceive you is unhealthy and prevents you from being your truest self.

Set out to do one thing you love that absolutely, positively brings you joy. Do it to inspire the people around you to be their authentic selves, too!

DARE TO INCLUDE GIRLS IN SPORTS

THINK BACK TO WHEN YOU WERE YOUNGER. DID YOU PLAY SPORTS with girls, either just for fun or on an organized team? Maybe it was soccer or basketball on the playground. Why, do you think, do boys typically play sports only with other boys after a certain age?

Well, it's because boys are taught to view girls as less athletic, talented, or aggressive than they are. Which could make you think girls are weak. That can't be true—just look at powerhouse female athletes like Serena Williams, Megan Rapinoe, Diana Taurasi, and Simone Biles.

The next time you and your boys are playing sports in the park or at recess, invite some girls to join you. And anytime they ask to play, always welcome them to your team. Don't be surprised if you find your new go-to guard or a fierce goalkeeper.

DARE TO
STAND UP FOR
SOMEONE WHO IS
BEING BULLIED

>>>———<<<

KIDS ARE BULLIED FOR A LOT OF REASONS, AND IT'S USUALLY because something about them is labeled "different." We've all, at certain points in our lives, felt out of place or like we didn't belong. Imagine feeling that way con-stantly.

When you see someone being bullied, it can be scary. You don't want the person to be hurt, and you also might be afraid to step in and become the bully's next target. Speaking up isn't easy, but if you do it, others will, too. If you see someone being bullied and you don't feel safe intervening in the moment, check with that person afterward. Let them know they're not alone: Ask to sit with them during lunch and at other times (assemblies, for example) when they might not have someone to hang out with. Offer to help them talk to a trusted adult, such as a teacher or parent. Be the friend you'd want to have if you were in their shoes.

DARE TO ENCOURAGE SOMEONE'S UNIQUENESS

SPEAKING OF DIFFERENCES . . . LET'S CELEBRATE THEM! HOW many times have you witnessed someone getting picked on for something totally harmless that affects literally no one else? It could be anything from a physical feature to the way they speak or choose to dress. People pick on others who they think are "unusual," when really they're just unique (a better word, and one that we prefer). Think about your closest friends and all the reasons you like them. Probably pretty specific reasons, right? We're not all meant to be the same. We're meant to be a supercool, uber-assorted group of people.

Be on the lookout for what makes someone special, and go out of your way to encourage it. Also spend some time thinking about the qualities that make *you* unique, and then embrace them with all you've got. Life would be so boring if we were all the same. Diversity is dope.

DARE TO
BE EMPOWERED

DO YOU EVER LET SOMEONE ELSE KEEP DOING SOMETHING FOR you, even if you're capable of doing it yourself? Maybe it's making that delicious turkey sandwich your parents pack for your lunch, washing your laundry, or organizing your closet. Even if someone has always offered to do those things for you, knowing how to do them yourself and becoming self-sufficient are even *more* empowering. And it's meaningful to help out a parent or friend because it makes their life easier.

This week, dare to do something on your own. Bonus points if it's something that'll not only benefit you, but also benefit others. Don't just put your clothes in the laundry—ask if someone else in your family needs something washed as well!

DARE TO SHARE YOUR TRUE FEELINGS

"HEY! HOW ARE YOU?" "I'M GOOD. YOU?"

How many times have you had this exact exchange? It's a common question with an even more common (and generic) answer. Are you really fine? Boys are taught not to share their feelings. You may have been taught that it's weak to ask for help. This means that "fine" is usually an answer for just about every feeling under the sun. Or a cover-up for something tough you're going through.

As hard as it can be, try not to run from your feelings. The next time someone asks how you're doing, challenge yourself to share the truth. Tell that friend or parent how you're frustrated, worried, upset, excited, anxious, or really happy. Explain why. It feels good to share your feelings openly, and if you're looking for help, the person you're talking to can offer insight.

DARE TO COMPLIMENT SOMEONE EVERY DAY

DO YOU EVER WISH THERE WERE MORE HOURS IN THE DAY?
One minute you're hitting the snooze button and the next you're setting the alarm for tomorrow. What gives?! Life can be challenging. Most days, you're walking a very thin tightrope as you balance your many responsibilities without forgetting homework or being late to activities, and while trying to have a social life, keep up on social media, and make sure everything is cool with Mom or Dad. Do you ever feel unseen or unheard in the chaos of everyday life? How would you feel if, during a hectic day, someone let you know you were doing something well?

Each day for one week, make a point to bring joy into someone else's life. Cheer them on, text them, send an email, or go old-school and call them to let them know they're doing a good job. When we shine a light on someone, that light is bound to shine back on us.

DARE TO
SUPPORT A GIRL
IN SCHOOL

DID YOU KNOW THAT, ON AVERAGE, TEACHERS SPEND UP TO TWO-thirds of their time talking to boys versus one-third to girls? And yet . . . boys are still more likely to interrupt girls when they're answering questions or sharing opinions in class. It's important to give equal time to everyone's voices, including girls—otherwise, you're participating in something called unconscious bias, and that's not fair.

What can you do to actively support girls in school? It can be as easy as saying "That's a good idea," or "I've never thought of it that way," or "She has a really good idea for a science project." The possibilities are endless! Just let the kindness flow.

DARE TO
START A JOURNAL

OUR SOCIETY HAS A BAD HABIT OF LABELING THINGS AS "FOR boys" and "for girls," but there's no reason behind it. Keeping a journal or diary is not naturally more "boy" or more "girl." Journals and diaries don't have a gender—they're literally notebooks with paper in them. And they're fantastic for keeping track of your very busy life and how things are going for you. Writing about your day can help clear your head and make important connections between your thoughts, actions, and feelings. Don't feel limited to a pen-and-paper journal, either. You can write on a computer, on a tablet, in an app, or in your phone's notes section. Heck, write on a gum wrapper if that's what you've got!

Starting tonight, write down a few things you remember from your day. If it feels too scary to write in full sentences or paragraphs, create lists instead. Write down three things you saw today—like a slice of pizza. Or five things you're grateful for—like that slice of pizza. At the end of the week, look back and see if anything stands out or surprises you. How was Friday different from Monday? The best part is that journals are for your eyes only—be as honest as you want.

DARE TO TRY A SPORT OR ACTIVITY THAT'S OUTSIDE YOUR COMFORT ZONE

WHETHER YOU'RE PART OF A TEAM, AN INDIVIDUAL SPORT, OR a group activity, we know you give your all. You work hard. You show up to your rehearsals or practices. You put everything you've got into it. (The rest—how many points you rack up, whether you win or lose—should pale in comparison.) But how often have you wanted to try a new sport or activity, only to stop yourself because you were afraid? Maybe you were worried that you wouldn't be a pro right off the bat. Or that your friends would laugh at you. Boys often get teased or mocked when they branch out and explore activities that aren't aggressive or tough enough.

If you never leave your comfort zone, you'll miss out on some pretty cool stuff. The next time you're interested in something new, pay attention to your gut—and don't be afraid to go for it! You might just discover that you *are* a natural at the least-expected thing.

DARE TO
BE A LEADER

WHAT DOES BEING A LEADER MEAN TO YOU? DOES THE TITLE *leader* feel like big shoes to fill—as if it can only be applied to the president or prime minister of a country? Well, it doesn't have to! There are so many ways to be a leader. Sometimes it can mean taking an important role in student government, on your sports team, or in drama class. Other times, it means doing things that show what's important to you—like recycling to protect the environment, selling candy to raise money for a local pet shelter, or volunteering at a nursing home. Even though the idea of *leading* can make you think of being strong and forceful, listening to other people, encouraging different opinions, and challenging old ideas are also ways of leading.

Dare to embrace leadership this year. Write down the ways you want to be a leader in your home, school, or community and dare to do the things on that list.

DARE TO
NAME THREE EMOTIONS
YOU FELT TODAY

DID YOU KNOW THAT THERE ARE *DOZENS* OF EMOTIONS? THE LIST gets pretty specific! But generally, we think of the major ones as anger, fear, sadness, disgust, surprise, anticipation, trust, and joy. Of these eight, how many have you felt recently?

Dare to jot down at least three emotions you felt today and how they affected you. For example, if you felt joy, what was the cause? Being able to identify your feelings will help you seek out the things that help you have positive emotions (like surprise, anticipation, trust, and joy), as well as how to handle the more difficult ones (like anger, fear, sadness, and disgust). This understanding makes up your emotional literacy, which is like a big book of tips and tricks that will help you express exactly how you feel and help you be a better problem solver.

DARE TO
INCLUDE SOMEONE
WHO IS LEFT OUT

YOU KNOW THAT FEELING WHEN YOU WALK INTO A PARTY AND you don't know anyone there? Or it's lunchtime and you don't see anyone to sit with? Maybe your friends are running late and you're the first one to arrive. Or perhaps you're brand-new to the scene. Some people have a knack for walking up to others and making new friends easily, but others need a little more time to feel comfortable. And both of those are okay.

Look around and notice who in the room is rolling solo. Walk over and start a conversation or invite them to join you at lunch or at the mall. If you're not sure what to say, start with a simple "hello." You never know who'll surprise you.

DARE TO BE INSPIRED BY DIVERSE STORIES AND AUTHORS

WHAT'S THE LATEST GREAT NOVEL, COMIC BOOK, GRAPHIC NOVEL, autobiography, or story you read? Who was the author? Where are they from? What are they writing about? Think about the stories you read for school and for fun. Do those stories include people of all genders, races, identities, and backgrounds—especially ones that are different from yours?

Dare to learn more about people who come from all walks of life. Next time you're browsing in a bookstore or reading for fun, choose an author whose story isn't like your own. It's sure to broaden your perspective, inspire new ideas, and help you think of different ways to overcome obstacles in your life.

DARE TO
TALK ABOUT A TIME
YOU WERE FRIGHTENED

MOST OF US ARE AFRAID OF SOMETHING. WHETHER IT'S A LESS serious thing like horror movies or spiders or thinking too long about outer space, or a more serious issue like losing a loved one or disappointing a friend—there's bound to be something that frightens you. Do you recall the last time you were afraid? Did you keep it to yourself or tell someone how you felt? The Man Box convinces boys that they always have to be in control and completely fearless. But scary things happen all the time, and everyone needs to be able to talk about them.

Think about a time when you were afraid—waking up from a nightmare, seeing something on the news, after an incident at school, during an argument at home, or because of something totally ridiculous but still legit scary to you—and talk about it with someone today. Acknowledging your feelings is the first step to overcoming your fears.

DARE TO
PROVE A STEREOTYPE
WRONG

A STEREOTYPE IS A SUPER-SIMPLE IDEA OR IMAGE OF A PERSON or thing based on the lowest common denominator. Like: *Oh, you're a boy? Then you must be the class clown; the strong, silent type; the big shot; or the action hero.* But you're more than that. There are many stereotypes about race, gender, age, religion, and ethnicity. The Man Box creates stereotypes that men and boys feel pressured to uphold, like the ones we've listed above.

This week, prove a stereotype wrong. Show that you're smart, sensitive, caring, and thoughtful. Being an action hero is cool—but you don't need to dodge burning cars or run to the rescue to prove you're brave. Instead, reach out to a friend or neighbor and offer your time to help them with something.

DARE TO
WATCH A MOVIE ABOUT
A GIRL OR A WOMAN

DO YOU EVER SEE A TRAILER FOR A MOVIE AND THINK, *HMM, that's not for me,* because it's a movie "for girls"? Remember: there's no such thing! Movies that center around the stories of other genders are not off-limits to you. Girls are just as interesting as boys. Girls and women can have superpowers and be the heroes of their own action films just as much as they can fall in love in dramas and make people laugh in comedies. Women have not always been represented positively in film and television. But that's changing, thanks in part to boys like you who go to see them in the theaters or watch at home.

So the next time you're texting the group chat and picking out a Friday night film or something to stream, do a little extra research. Kick back, grab the popcorn and your favorite candy, and prepare to be entertained as you enjoy movies about and made by women.

DARE TO
COMFORT A FRIEND

THERE'S AN IRISH SAYING THAT GOES LIKE THIS: "THERE ARE good ships and wood ships and ships that sail the sea. But the best ships are friendships and may they always be." If you have really good close friends, you know that friendship feels a lot like finding gold at the end of a rainbow. Have you ever seen one of those friends, or even a classmate, upset and going through a hard time, but you felt too awkward to get involved? Maybe you didn't know what to say or thought you wouldn't be able to help. Being there for a friend can be as simple as asking if they want to talk. You don't need to have the solution to their problems. You don't even have to have *any* answer. They probably don't expect you to, anyway. Sometimes listening is all they need, because it shows that you care.

Keep your eyes—and ears—open this week. If one of your friends or family members is upset, show them they can trust you by comforting them. Listen to them as they open up to you and remember that just being there is enough.

DARE TO
LISTEN TO A PODCAST
OR AN AUDIOBOOK
ABOUT SOMEONE WHO IS
DIFFERENT FROM YOU

ONE OF THE GREATEST ATTRIBUTES BOYS CAN LEARN IS EMPATHY. People often get empathy and sympathy confused, but the two are different. Sympathy is compassion for someone in a tough situation. But empathy—that's when you put yourself in someone else's shoes and try to really feel what they're experiencing.

The next time you put your headphones on or your earbuds in, try selecting a podcast or audiobook instead of your usual music playlist. While it's more than okay to seek out stories that reflect your own experiences, look beyond, too, and find stories about people, places, and events that are different and unknown. If you live in a city, try stories from the country. If you come from a family that doesn't have to worry about money, read about someone who's had a harder time paying the bills. Listen to stories about girls, little-known historical figures—any group of people who are often overlooked. It's daring to broaden your experience and empathize with people who are different from you.

DARE TO
COOK FOR SOMEONE

WHAT ARE YOUR FAVORITE COMFORT FOODS? YOU KNOW, THE meals guaranteed to make you feel better when you're sick or having a tough day? A grilled cheese sandwich and soup come to mind. Or maybe you like something that makes everyone else think *Huh?* but you know it's a cure-all. Food has the power to connect us and can bring so much joy—you know what that first bite of a really good sandwich tastes like. Food is also nourishing, and we need it to, you know, live.

Cooking for someone is a way to show you care. The Man Box tries to tell boys that they shouldn't take care of others—that nurturing is for girls. But boys are caring, too. You don't want to see someone you care about sick and in pain. This week, cook for someone who's sick or having a terrible, horrible, no-good, very bad day. It doesn't have to be fancy—remember, grilled cheese or scrambled eggs is often a favorite!

DARE TO
MAKE A NEW FRIEND
WHO DOESN'T
LOOK LIKE YOU

OPEN UP YOUR PHONE AND SCROLL THROUGH RECENT PICS OF YOUR friends. What does your group look like? Open up your most recent yearbook and flip through the pages. What does your school look like? Are you all mostly alike—meaning people of the same gender and race and from the same part of town? Or, when you look around, are you all pretty different?

Being part of a group that has lots of diversity makes you a well-rounded friend and a more confident person. It's also just fun to branch out and experience different cultures and traditions, try new foods, and listen to unfamiliar kinds of music. Try to make a new friend this semester who maybe doesn't look like you or share the same experiences, but who you'd like to get to know better.

DARE TO
CREATE A VISION BOARD
FOR YOUR LIFE

WE BET THAT WHEN SOMEONE ASKS YOU WHERE YOU SEE YOUR-self in ten years, you have a lot of ideas. So, what are they? Do you want to travel somewhere new? Do you want to go to a community college, a four-year college, no college at all? Do you want to learn a trade, like working construction or becoming a barber? Do you want to be an engineer or a professional athlete or a teacher? Do you see yourself with a family? What other hopes and dreams do you have, and how do you think you'll achieve them?

Find a poster board or a big sheet of paper to use for your vision board. On it, map out your goals by drawing, cutting, pasting, and designing visuals that represent what you want in the future. Add photos of people and things you're really into now as well. There's no right or wrong way to create a vision board! It's your design, and its purpose is to help you set some goals and figure out how you'll reach them.

DARE TO
BE UNCOMFORTABLE

HAVE YOU EVER TRIED TO LEARN SOMETHING NEW, PRACTICED IT over and over again, and still not been able to get the hang of it? Or have you ever gotten into a fierce debate or argument with a friend and both of you were too stubborn and hotheaded to compromise? Maybe you've tried to get good at a musical instrument, or score as many points as possible in a video game, and yet no matter how hard you try, you just can't get there. In every case, you've reached a point where you want to give up and walk away. The moment you want to throw your hands up in surrender is uncomfortable, frustrating, and really hard. But it's not necessarily the end.

This week, dare to embrace being uncomfortable. Stare down that challenge standing in your way and try your best to push through it so you can level up.

DARE TO
GO TO A GIRLS'
SPORTING EVENT

WOULD YOUR FRIENDS JOIN YOU TO WATCH A GIRLS' SOFTBALL, basketball, or soccer game? What about a viewing party for the WNBA Finals? Why do you think girls' and women's sports are pushed aside and not given as much attention as boys' and men's sports—even in cases when the women's team has won more games? Men's sports may seem more exciting, but that's because there's more investment in them—celebrity commentary and fancier television production.

This week, go out and support a girls' sporting event at your school or in your community. Get a group of friends together to come with you, and root for your team from the benches, bleachers, and sidelines!

DARE TO
TEACH A FRIEND
SOMETHING YOU'RE
GOOD AT

CAN YOU SOLVE A RUBIK'S CUBE? CAN YOU MAKE AN AMAZING omelet? Fold an origami frog that leaps or make a paper airplane that flies? Maybe you can draw just about anything. Sometimes it feels uncomfortable—intimidating, even—for boys to share things they're good at because it means showing a special part of themselves they don't want anyone to reject. That feeling is called vulnerability, and it's one type of emotional exposure. No doubt about it: vulnerability can be scary! But it leads to good things, like connecting more closely with others. It takes a whole lot of courage to put yourself out there.

Be brave this week and commit to teaching a close friend how to do something you're good at. Not only will they learn something new, but you'll have another person to enjoy it with you!

DARE TO VOLUNTEER WITH A PROGRAM FOR PEOPLE WHO HAVE PHYSICAL, DEVELOPMENTAL, OR OTHER CHALLENGES

IT'S SO EASY FOR ABLE-BODIED PEOPLE TO TAKE FOR GRANTED things that come naturally to them—running down the street or listening to music. But many people live with visible and invisible challenges. Visible challenges are things you can see, like needing a wheelchair or using a crutch. Other challenges—like being hearing-impaired or having a learning disability—aren't visible on the surface, but that doesn't make them any less valid.

Have you ever felt unsure of how to act around someone who doesn't have the same abilities as you do? That feeling of uncertainty often comes from simply not having enough experience. Our goal is to make sure that everyone, no matter their physical and mental capabilities, feels comfortable. This year, volunteer some time with an organization like the Special Olympics or Easterseals and get to know people with different kinds of challenges.

DARE TO START AN EXERCISE ROUTINE

EXERCISE IS ONE OF THE BEST WAYS TO TAKE CARE OF YOUR BODY and stay healthy. It's also been scientifically proven to make you feel happier, because all that movement releases chemicals into your body that fight feelings of sluggishness and sadness.

This month, dare to start a consistent exercise routine. You can go to the gym and work out on your own, get help from a trainer, ride your bike, go for a run, go to the park, or simply climb up and down bleachers or stairs. Commit for four weeks and compare how you feel in the beginning to your mood at the end. You may just want to keep going. Taking care of your body is a win!

DARE TO WRITE A LETTER TO SOMEONE WHO INSPIRES YOU

IS THERE SOMEONE IN YOUR LIFE WHO MAKES YOU WANT TO BE better at something? Maybe it's acting, sports, art, school, or something totally new and different that person has mastered. Or do you look up to a coach, a teacher, a young activist, or a leader in your community? There are so many hardworking and creative people using their influence to make the world a better place.

Think about the people who inspire you most, talk with a parent about them, and dare to write to them. In your message, express why their work is meaningful to you and what you've learned from them. No matter how well known someone becomes, it's always gratifying for them to know they're making a positive impact on someone. Plus, you never know what might happen as a result of taking fifteen minutes out of your busy day to send a note.

DARE TO
ASK GIRLS TO
HANG OUT—JUST
AS FRIENDS

WHEN BOYS START SCHOOL, THEY'RE SOMETIMES TAUGHT NOT TO be interested in girls unless they like them—you know, as in "like-like" them. Believe it or not, boys and girls *can* develop close friendships, and you can like a girl without like-liking her.

Try asking girls questions you'd want to answer yourself. What was your favorite vacation? What are you binge-watching now? What's your favorite food? By learning about the lives of girls—as friends—you'll come to realize there's a lot more to them than what you see in school. You may even shock yourself by finding out that you have a lot in common! It's the start of strengthening your friendships and growing into a well-rounded person. And it will help you be ready to stand up for girls when they're being treated unfairly.

DARE TO
LOVE YOURSELF

SOMETIMES WE'RE WAY TOO HARD ON OURSELVES. IF SOMETHING goes wrong, it's easy to think, *If only I had done this better!* or *Why can't I be as good as him?* Remember that there's a whole list of things that make you uniquely . . . you! Your love of music, your facial features, your body, your gift for math, your love of animals—literally *all* the things about you.

Write down that list and then dare to love and appreciate all those things for a week, or a day, or at least an hour. Look in the mirror and say, "I love that I'm good at math." It's going to feel weird and maybe even a little braggy, but what you say to yourself affects how you feel about yourself. Saying something like "I love that I'm good at math" is called an affirmation, and we want to keep the things we say to ourselves as positive—as *affirmative*—as possible. It all starts with you: liking and being nice to yourself means you'll be able to do the same for others.

DARE TO
HELP AROUND THE
HOUSE AND EXPECT
NO REWARD

VACUUMING. DUSTING. MOPPING. WASHING THE WINDOWS. DO these chores strike terror, or maybe intense boredom, into your heart? So much so that your parents give you an allowance for helping with them? When a family member asks for your help, is your first thought: *What am I going to get for doing this?* The reality is that not everyone gets paid to pitch in around the house—after all, it's where you live, too—and one day you'll have to do many of these chores by yourself, without any extra incentive.

Dare to help out without being offered any reward. You might surprise yourself with how good it feels to get something done without money attached to it.

DARE TO
ASK FOR HELP

ONE OF THE MOST DIFFICULT THINGS TO DO IN LIFE IS TO ASK for help. How many times have you struggled with something—homework, something someone said, an argument with your parents—but felt uncomfortable asking for help? You're not alone. The Man Box teaches boys that reaching out and asking for help is a sign of weakness. No one should have to solve their toughest problems by themselves. Everybody needs help, and it's important to remember that asking for it doesn't make you any less of a boy. In fact, being vulnerable and asking for help is one of the bravest things a person can do and is surely a sign of strength.

The next time you're struggling with something big or small, dare to ask a trusted friend or adult for help. Almost one hundred percent of the time, it'll save you a lot of extra worry and stress. And just think what you can do with all that extra time on your hands!

DARE TO
SAY THANK YOU
IF SOMEONE PRAISES
OR COMPLIMENTS YOU

HOW DO YOU REACT WHEN SOMEONE SAYS SOMETHING NICE about you? Do you downplay what they've said, replying with something like "No way" or "Well, not as good as you" or "Come on, man"? We know it can be hard to feel and express confidence without worrying that you look like you're flexing. But there's a difference between confidence and cockiness, and you shouldn't worry that accepting a compliment will make you come off as having a huge ego.

The next time someone lifts you up and praises you, pay attention to how you react. Are you deflecting? Rather than fighting it, practice saying a simple "Thank you" and leaving it at that. Then pass it on and compliment someone else around you.

DARE TO
WASH AND DRY THE
DISHES FOR A WEEK

WHO'S RESPONSIBLE FOR DOING THE DISHES IN YOUR HOUSEHOLD?

Who do you think does them most often? Traditionally, girls and women are stuck with this chore, as if they should always be the ones cleaning up. People may not see cleaning up in the kitchen as one of your responsibilities because you're a boy. And this goes beyond loading dishes into the dishwasher. Sometimes you might have to roll up your sleeves and do the dishes by hand.

Helping around the house is a great way to show people your true character—that you're responsible, that you're a team player, and that you know how to take care of things at home. Instead of letting a machine or someone else you know do the dishes, volunteer to step in and do them yourself for a week.

DARE TO
BREAK DOWN
THE MAN BOX

THE PHRASE *MAN BOX* DESCRIBES THE NOT-SO-GREAT WAYS IN which boys are taught to be men. The Man Box tells boys that they should be strong, and that they're not allowed to be afraid or to cry. Too often, the Man Box can hold boys back—it's much too limiting. Boys are multilayered human beings with a bunch of great qualities that make them good people.

This week, dare to break down the Man Box. Draw a box. Inside the box, write down the ways you have felt pressured to "man up," which is something boys are often told. Outside the box, write down all the things you love or enjoy that don't fit into the box. Focus on the words you've written outside the box and incorporate those qualities and activities into your everyday life so you can lead a healthy life.

DARE TO
SHOW YOU CARE

SOMETIMES THE PEOPLE WE LOVE MAKE CHOICES THAT AREN'T good for them. We know that smoking and vaping can cause serious harm and even lead to lung cancer. And despite the dangers of texting while driving, people still look away from the road to send a message or two. It can be scary to think about the consequences of those actions affecting a friend or family member. The thought of talking to that same friend or family member and asking them to make a change can be scary, too. But bottling up that frustration and fear can lead to arguments.

When the time feels right, be brave and talk to a loved one about a habit that worries you. Let them know you're bringing it up because you care and don't want anything bad to happen to them. Showing your concern might lead them to make a meaningful change in their lives.

DARE TO
TRY A NEW HAIRCUT

EVER FEEL THE NEED TO MIX UP YOUR STYLE? HAVE YOU SECRETLY wanted to try a new haircut or hair color for a while now? Don't let the fear of looking different stop you. There are so many possibilities when it comes to switching things up. Just go for it!

Dare to make a change. Ask your parents and share some ideas with your barber or stylist. Try a temporary color that shampoos out. Save pictures of trendy cuts you might want to try for yourself. Embrace your natural texture. Grow it out. Shave it all off. It's your crowning glory, after all! Mixing it up and exploring your personal style is a fun way to express your authenticity and individuality.

DARE TO
BE AN ASPIRING ALLY

THESAURUS TIME! DO YOU NEED ANOTHER WORD FOR *FRIEND*? We've got your back. *Ally* means the same thing. And an aspiring ally is someone who wants to be a friend to a group of people who aren't always treated fairly.

Dare to be an aspiring ally and stand in solidarity with people of backgrounds, races, and genders who are often treated unfairly. Listen to their ideas on how to make things better, and ask them how you can help support those ideas. It's not easy, and it's okay if you make mistakes while navigating issues that might be new to you. Your heart is in the right place, and your friends will recognize that. That's why it's called aspiring, anyway—because you keep trying to be your best.

DARE TO WEAR A FEMALE PROFESSIONAL ATHLETE'S JERSEY

WHEN WE WEAR TEAM GEAR, IT LETS THE WORLD KNOW WHO AND what we stand for. Having a name on your back takes it even further. Whether your jersey reads James, Mahomes, Messi, or Harper, you're telling your friends you've got mad love for that player. Do you extend that same respect and support to female professional athletes?

Commit to showing up as an ally for girls by wearing the jersey of a female professional athlete you admire. Wearing their gear will give you a natural way to talk about how great they are, and ultimately, make them more popular players.

DARE TO
USE YOUR PRONOUN
WHEN INTRODUCING
YOURSELF

HAVE YOU EVER SEEN OR HEARD SOMEONE ON TELEVISION OR social media introduce themselves with their name and their pronoun—he, she, or they? That person is sharing the pronoun they choose to use. You can't always know what someone's pronoun is by looking at them. Asking and correctly using someone's preferred pronoun is a basic way to show your respect for their gender identity. And if you mistakenly use the wrong pronoun for someone, just acknowledge your mistake, apologize, and move on.

The next time you introduce yourself to someone, dare to use your pronoun and try asking them: "What are your preferred pronouns?"

DARE TO
DO SOMETHING KIND
JUST BECAUSE

HAVE YOU EVER DONE SOMETHING NICE FOR SOMEONE WITHOUT them knowing you were behind it? It's such a great feeling to witness their joy and quietly know you created that moment. Or have you ever done something helpful without feeling the need to tell everyone about it? It's super satisfying to know you've chipped in somewhere without taking credit for it.

Dare to perform one random act of kindness each week. Remember that it doesn't have to be something time-consuming or BIG. You can let someone go ahead of you in line, pay for someone's snack, pick up litter, give someone a gift without expecting one in return, send a card or a friendly text, or do something completely original!

DARE TO
TELL SOMEONE THEY
MATTER TO YOU

WHO LIKES REJECTION? NO ONE. IT'S SCARY, IT'S AWFUL, AND IT makes us feel like we're less than. That's why most people are afraid to share their true feelings. We avoid being honest and vulnerable because we don't want to risk being turned down. At the same time, there are amazingly important people in our lives who love us no matter what. These people are invested in our happiness. We owe those people a little love back. They should know how much they matter to us.

Find a way this week to tell someone how happy you are to know them, and that they make a difference in your life. Chat with them in person, write a text, or even give them a handwritten note—whatever way you want to express your gratitude for them.

DARE TO
SPEND TIME WITH A
REAL-LIFE ROLE MODEL

IS THERE SOMEONE IN YOUR LIFE THAT YOU LOOK UP TO? MAYBE it's your dad, brother, grandfather, uncle . . . maybe it's your mom, sister, grandmother, aunt, a coach, or a teacher you want to be like when you're older. There are many celebrities, A-listers, and influencers we admire, but what about the not-so-famous people in our lives who make an impact on the daily?

Dare to think of heroes and role models as the people you know and not necessarily the ones you see on television. Reach out to them and ask if you can meet up. You might learn something from them, and they might surprise you by saying they look up to you, too.

DARE TO
EAT MORE HEALTHILY

MOST OF US DON'T SPEND A WHOLE LOT OF TIME THINKING ABOUT our overall health until something goes wrong. But that advice to eat more veggies and cut the sugar is actually a really good thing. Eating healthily and exercising will help you grow better and stronger, so why not begin now?

Dare to change something about your diet this week—big or small—that will help make you healthier. It could be adding a new food item, cutting something out, or maybe adjusting another eating habit that you've already been working on. Better yet, do it with a friend so you can help each other along!

DARE TO
SAY "I'M SORRY"

IT CAN BE HARD TO SAY "I'M SORRY." IT MEANS WE'RE ADMITTING to something we've done wrong. Of course, none of us go out of our way to purposefully mistreat someone or hurt their feelings, but even if we didn't mean to upset someone, the impact of our actions is what matters most. If someone says they're hurt, believe them. Everyone makes mistakes—everyone. And at many points in our lives, we'll be on both the giving and the receiving ends of apologies.

When we've hurt someone—even by accident—it's important to listen to them, to try to understand how we hurt them, and to bravely say "I'm sorry." Holding ourselves accountable for our actions and how we've affected people around us will make us better friends and members of our families and communities.

DARE TO
SAY "I'M AFRAID"

WHEN YOU'RE SCARED OF SOMETHING, HOW WOULD YOU DESCRIBE that feeling? You're probably thinking: *I'd describe it as "scared," duh.* But we've talked to some adult men who break it down further as feeling stressed out, concerned, or worried. When they were your age, the Man Box taught them that, once again, feeling anything other than brave and strong all the time was a weakness, even though scary things happen all the time. So let yourself be vulnerable and say it out loud to someone you trust: "I'm afraid." Just by saying it, you will start to feel better and less alone.

DARE TO
BE AN INFLUENCER

WHETHER IT'S WITH YOUR FRIENDS, YOUR CLASSMATES, OR YOUR family, you have the ability to affect people's thoughts and actions. That means you have influence. Have you ever thought about the ways you can use your influence to make positive changes in the world? Maybe you're really good at recycling and want to help show other people how easy it is. Or maybe you want to bring attention to a social issue like bullying. Doing something good can create a ripple effect: if you demonstrate for one person the good you're doing, there's an excellent chance they'll be inspired to share some goodness with the next person. Start that chain reaction!

Make a list of the groups of people you can influence and the things you care deeply about, and dare to think about how you want to use that influence for good.

DARE TO
TRY HARD

HAVE YOU EVER BEEN IN CLASS AND REALLY WANTED TO DO WELL on an assignment but didn't want to show it? That's because the Man Box teaches you not to care all that much about studying and that you should just handle whatever comes your way or you might be called nerdy (as if there's something wrong with being book-smart! SMH). Maybe you didn't understand a new math unit, but you didn't want to ask for help and you did poorly on the test, so now you're grounded for getting a bad grade. Had you just asked for help, you could have prevented all that trouble—don't let those trying to look cool set you on a harmful path.

Next time you have an opportunity to excel, go for it! And if you hit a roadblock along the way, don't be afraid to ask for help, try a little harder, and push toward success.

DARE TO
LISTEN TO FEMALE
MUSICAL ARTISTS

OPEN ONE OF YOUR PLAYLISTS AND CHECK OUT YOUR GO-TO artists. Count how many are male. How many are female or don't express themselves in ways typically considered masculine or feminine? Notice anything? Today, only two out of every ten recording artists in almost every musical genre, including hip-hop, rock, pop, country, and dance, are women. By supporting women and gender-nonconforming artists, you can help them succeed.

Dare to have a different musical experience and listen to female or gender-nonconforming musicians for a week. By streaming or purchasing music by these artists, you'll be supporting their talent and gaining insight into others' perspectives while also broadening your own.

DARE TO
HANG OUT WITH
SOMEONE NEW

HAVE YOU EVER BEEN THE NEW KID? EVEN IF YOU HAVEN'T, YOU probably know what it's like to be the odd one out, waiting for someone to come over and talk to you. It can be especially hard if you don't look like anyone else in the room. It takes one person saying hi to make someone feel included. One wave or hand gesture for them to come over, hang out, and feel less weird. One invitation to a movie to make that lonely, nervous feeling go away.

Whenever you see someone new, dare to be inclusive and ask them to hang out. You may just hit it off and make an entirely new friend . . . all thanks to simply saying hello.

DARE TO
START A WEEKLY
HANGOUT

DO YOU AND YOUR FRIENDS GET TOGETHER REGULARLY TO PLAY video games? Or maybe you like to see a movie or watch a ball game? What if you made those activities a regular thing and used that time to talk about some of the ideas in this book? You can choose dares to do as a group or do them solo and then all check in together the following week. Checking in each week will help keep all of you accountable, track your progress, and—best of all—make your friendships tighter than ever.

DARE TO
SAY "I DON'T KNOW"

YOU KNOW THOSE KIDS WHO HAVE AN ANSWER FOR EVERYTHING? The ones who'll double or even triple down on something just to avoid saying "I don't know"? Have you ever completely made up an answer to avoid looking dumb? Boys are taught they should always be in charge, and part of that is not just knowing the answer, but knowing the *right* answer. Boys feel an unfair amount of pressure to know it all, which is impossible.

Understanding that you don't have to have all the answers will help you live a healthy and happy life. Dare to be okay with saying "I don't know," and listen and learn from others.

DARE TO
HELP SOMEONE WITHOUT
HAVING TO BE ASKED

AS YOU KNOW BY NOW, BOYS ARE HESITANT TO ASK FOR AND accept help. But it can also be difficult to *offer* help if someone doesn't directly ask for it. If you see someone struggling to open a door, to carry all their books to class, or to cross the street with groceries, do you rush in to assist because they need a helping hand? Or do you wait to be asked?

Each day this week, find a way to help someone. If a friend is stressing about rehearsals, offer to run lines with them. If an older person lives in your neighborhood, ask if you can help with chores around their yard or house. Dare to help lighten the load for someone and be proud of being a helper.

DARE TO
CHIP IN FOR EQUAL PAY

IMAGINE THIS: YOU AND YOUR SISTER ARE ASKED TO TAKE TURNS doing the dishes each night for a month. At the end of the month, your parents promise to pay you both. Thirty days later, your sister is paid $30, but you only get $27. You did the exact same amount of work and did an equally good job, but she got more. How would that make you feel? Did you know that women are paid less than men for doing the same job? And that women who are Black and Latina are paid even less than white women? That's called the wage gap, and it's just one example of how women are valued less than men.

This week, ask your parents if the places they work pay women the same as men. Talk about what you can do as a family to help make pay equal.

DARE TO
TALK ABOUT SOMETHING
YOU'RE PROUD OF

THINK ABOUT YOUR LATEST, GREATEST ACHIEVEMENT. WAS IT A trophy or a medal you won? A test you aced? Something you cooked, baked, built, or created? How awesome did it feel to accomplish or produce it? Probably pretty dang good, yeah? Now think back to what happened after. Did you share your triumph with a friend or a family member? Were you able to talk about the things that made it challenging and rewarding?

Boys are taught that they shouldn't care too much—that they should always play it cool. No more of that! This week, dare to celebrate something you're especially proud of. And if someone helped you achieve that success, make sure to thank them, too.

DARE TO SPEAK OUT ON A CAUSE THAT MATTERS TO YOU

IS THERE AN ISSUE THAT MEANS A LOT TO YOU? MAYBE IT'S climate change, the treatment of immigrants, or equal pay for men and women. Even though you might not be old enough to vote, it's never too early to start voicing your concerns and ideas to your local, state, and national representatives. You can write to your mayor, governor, state senator, or congressperson. Youth activists just like you are absolutely capable of making meaningful changes in the world. After all, you're the future!

Dare to speak up and make big changes for the world you're living in—and the one your future family will inherit. Don't just follow in someone else's footsteps. Make your own!

DARE TO
BE A ROLE MODEL

YOU MIGHT NOT EVEN REALIZE IT, BUT YOU'RE A ROLE MODEL FOR someone! There are lots of young kids around you who are paying attention to their friends and classmates, which means you have an opportunity to set a good example and look out for them. That's the foundation of being a positive role model.

Dare to embrace your role and show up for the people who admire you. You can help younger siblings or friends with their homework, talk to them when they've had a bad day, and encourage them to believe in themselves . . . because *you* believe in them.

DARE TO
IDENTIFY YOUR GIFTS

>>>———<<<

WHEN IT COMES TO BEING GIFTED AT THINGS, THERE ARE TWO B-words that stop people from being proud of themselves: *boasting* and *bragging*. People worry that if they talk about being good at something, it'll come off as bigheaded and self-centered. But there's always a time and a place to be proud of your gifts! Do you know what yours are? Maybe you sing or rap. Maybe you're a good listener. Maybe you can swim and want to be a lifeguard one day. Perhaps you're really organized and your teachers are constantly impressed by your homework assignments.

Whatever your talents may be, dare to spend some time thinking about what you're good at and make a list of at least five things. Next to each one, write down a way you can use that gift to help others this week.

DARE TO
BE AN ACTIVE LISTENER

TALKING IS EASY. BUT LEARNING TO TRULY LISTEN TO SOMEONE IS an invaluable skill that will help you the rest of your life. Think about it: When someone's telling a story, are you listening with your undivided attention, or do you have the urge to interrupt all the time? Has someone had to say "Let me finish!" to you more than once in a conversation? If you're just waiting until it's your turn to talk, you're not really taking in everything your friend is saying. That can end up keeping you from really hearing what your friend, family member, teacher, or coach is trying to tell you. It's an easy way to miss what's important.

This week, dare to really listen and focus all your attention on what someone is sharing with you. Ask questions that add to the conversation and watch how your friends open up.

DARE TO THINK ABOUT A SONG'S LYRICS

MUSIC IS ONE OF THE MOST POWERFUL ART FORMS WE HAVE. IT can make us feel joyful, sad, angry, hyped up, or relaxed . . . all in under four minutes! Music is powerful, and it's everywhere—in our earbuds, in the car, at the mall, at concerts, and sometimes even at school activities. Professional athletes choose signature songs to walk out to. Actors walk up to accept awards with music playing behind them. Models walk down runways to musical beats.

But do you ever stop to listen to the message in a song? Take a screenshot of the lyrics to your favorite song and think about what they mean. Are there words, phrases, or imagery that rub you the wrong way? See if that changes how you think about that song or that artist.

DARE TO
GO TECH-FREE

IT'S HARD TO IMAGINE A WORLD WITHOUT TECHNOLOGY. BUT believe it or not, people did survive once upon a time without a screen in front of them 24-7. Technology is an awesome way to connect with people all over the world, play games when we're bored or on long road trips, and be part of special moments even if we're hundreds of miles away. Sometimes, though, that can feel overwhelming—like you have to check your messages every minute to avoid FOMO (you know, *fear of missing out*), or because you're afraid your friend will be upset if you don't respond to their texts or comment on their posts fast enough.

It's more important than ever to take short breaks from screens. Dare to go tech-free for a whole day and see how you feel. Go completely offline. Turn off your phone and don't check it until the next morning. It's okay to let your friends know—maybe they can join you in unplugging.

DARE TO
ASK A GIRL WHAT
SHE THINKS

YOU'VE HEARD OF A REPEAT, BUT WHAT ABOUT *HEPEAT*? WHEN A girl suggests an idea that gets ignored, only for a boy to say the exact same thing and suddenly everyone loves it . . . well, that's a hepeat. Sometimes girls' opinions aren't taken as seriously as boys' opinions, which teaches boys not to value girls' ideas. It's not your fault as an individual boy. It's something that has been passed down from one generation to the next and that many boys have to unlearn.

It happens more often than you think. Take notice when it does. Seek out ways to ask girls for their thoughts, listen to their suggestions, and give them credit when they come up with awesome new ideas.

DARE TO
CALL A DO-OVER

TIME OUT! HAVE YOU EVER WALKED AWAY FROM SPENDING TIME with your friends or talking with your family and really, really, *really* wished for a do-over because you said something in the moment you wish you hadn't? Sometimes when we look back, we wish we'd expressed ourselves or done something differently. But that's okay! Thinking about how we use our words and how we act is a great way to learn and grow. It takes vulnerability and courage to admit when you aren't your best self.

Dare to call a do-over this week if you walk away from an interaction that could have gone better.

DARE TO
BE THANKFUL

ONE VERY EASY, COST-EFFECTIVE WAY TO LIVE A HAPPY AND healthy life is to think about all the people, places, and things you're grateful for. It's basically like Thanksgiving every day but without the food. Finding things to be thankful for will make you feel better even on hard days—*especially* on hard days, when we need to be reminded of the good things that surround us. People who practice gratitude are generally healthier and more confident and even sleep better. And we could all use a few more z's at night.

This week, dare to start or end each day by jotting down three things you're thankful for. It can be as general (friends, siblings, sports teams) or as specific (new sneakers, a television show, a book) as you want, just as long as what you write brings you joy.

DARE TO
LEARN SOMETHING
NEW ABOUT YOURSELF

IS PURPLE YOUR GO-TO COLOR? DO YOU LOVE GAMING? AND skateboarding? Is band your favorite activity? Be you! Being authentic is about keeping it real—not pretending that your favorite color is blue when it's really orange. Being honest about who you are and what you like will make you happier and more confident. This week, dare to make a list of ten things that make you uniquely you! Think about when you felt most joyful or content, and remember what you were doing during those times. You might learn that painting makes you feel peaceful or fishing is your favorite—even if you only tried it that one time at summer camp.

DARE TO
SAY "I LOVE YOU"

EIGHT LETTERS. THREE SIMPLE WORDS. ONE SCARY PHRASE?

Saying "I love you" out loud is one of the hardest things for *anyone* to do, but especially for boys. The Man Box teaches you that sharing feelings is something only girls do. Saying "I love you" can be uncomfortable. Maybe in the past, saying it has felt too mushy? Or, *gulp,* too serious? But telling someone you love them *is* good for you, since it can make you happier, stronger, and healthier. Reminding family members and friends that they are loved will make them feel appreciated and cared for.

Right now, tomorrow, and for as many days going forward as possible, dare to say "I love you" to someone you care about and see how it makes them feel. There's a good chance they'll say it back. And it's always nice to feel the love.

DARE TO
CRY

CAN YOU REMEMBER THE LAST TIME YOU CRIED? WAS IT A FEW days ago? A week or a couple of months? Maybe even a year or more? Try really hard to concentrate and think back to that moment when you couldn't help but let the tears flow. Did you want to run away and hide your face? That feeling is called embarrassment, and it's a common reaction because the Man Box teaches boys that it's weak to cry. But you should never feel embarrassed about a little salt water leaking from your eyes. Crying is a natural and normal way to get rid of frustration and sadness. Sometimes that release is exactly what we need to move on and overcome our sadness.

The next time you're feeling overwhelmed and the tears begin to form, dare to cry and let those feelings out. Cry in private by yourself if that feels more comfortable, but also remember that you can cry with a close family member and friend if you're going through a rough patch. They won't judge you. They'll be there to support you.

DARE TO
NOT USE VIOLENT
LANGUAGE

TURN TO ANY TV CHANNEL OR OPEN A NEWS APP AND YOU'LL SEE a startling truth: violence is all around us. It's so common that a lot of the time we don't even notice it. And violence, unfortunately, comes in different shapes and sizes. Think about some of the things we say all the time: "That kills me." "Take a stab at it." "Beats me." "When push comes to shove." These sentences may seem innocent, but that's because they're so common they make the violent words in them feel ordinary. Do your siblings ever say "If you tell Dad, I'll kill you" or "I'm gonna rip your face off"? Those are pretty harsh words.

When we change the words we use, we also transform the way our brains process that information. This week, take notice when people around you use violent language—even mild-sounding language—and dare to stop saying them in your own conversations.

DARE TO
SAY "THAT'S NOT COOL"

THE PRESSURE TO FIT IN CAN BE SO OVERWHELMING THAT sometimes boys agree with things others say because it's easier than making noise. How many times have you witnessed someone saying something rude or acting in a mean-spirited way that you don't agree with, but you weren't sure what to do or say? Or maybe you did know what to say but you were too scared to step in. Sometimes if you see someone getting made fun of or you hear someone tell a hurtful joke, it can feel easier to look the other way. But being a bystander only makes things worse.

Make a pledge to start speaking up when you notice someone saying or doing something that could have a harmful outcome. Even if it feels awkward to say "That's not cool" or "Chill," dare to stand up for what's right.

DARE TO
CARE ABOUT THE
ENVIRONMENT

CAN YOU PICTURE YOURSELF AT EIGHTY YEARS OLD? DON'T WORRY, IT'S super far away. But stop for a minute to think about the fact that Earth is more than *four billion* years old. Can you imagine everything our planet has been through in that time? Back when the dinosaurs roamed, it was easier for the planet to stay healthy. There were no huge factories, massive buildings, homes, or cars pumping pollution into the air. Today, climate change is a very serious issue that not enough people are helping with. The Man Box tells boys they should dominate everyone and everything around them. Those harmful ideas even have an impact on the environment. Did you know that boys are more likely to litter and less likely to recycle because they don't want to "act like a girl"?

There are many ways we can help the planet, though, and if we each do our own small part, we can make a big impact. For example, do you recycle or pick up litter and trash when you see it fall on the ground? Dare to care about the environment you live in and the world around you. You can commit to recycling at home, carrying reusable tote bags instead of using plastic ones, drinking from a glass water bottle instead of a plastic one, and organizing an event to help clean up your local park or the block you live on.

DARE TO
GO TO A PRIDE EVENT
IN YOUR COMMUNITY

HAVE YOU EVER SEEN A RAINBOW FLAG IN A RESTAURANT OR store window and wondered what it means? The rainbow flag and its colors represent the diversity of the LGBTQ+ community, which stands for lesbian, gay, bisexual, transgender, queer+. The rainbow flag is a symbol of that community, which is why you see a lot of the flags during Pride parades and other festivities that celebrate love for and acceptance of people in that community.

This year, dare to support the LGBTQ+ community. Ask a parent if you can attend a Pride event. Show up and cheer them on. Look into joining a club at school. Seek out shows, movies, books, or podcasts that include people from that community. Your support will show that you're an ally to everyone.

DARE TO
NOT PUT GIRLS DOWN

SOME WORDS AND PHRASES DON'T NEED EXPLANATIONS—THEY'RE self-defining. Take, for instance, *put down*. It means making someone feel small, insignificant, and unimportant. How often have you heard phrases or words that put girls down? Even if you and your friends aren't using them, take a look at our culture. Some of the most-played songs are filled with lyrics that are disrespectful to girls and women. Plenty of popular shows and movies try to be funny by putting girls down. Think about what you've heard around you at school, at practice, or at the park. Because boys hear these things all the time, they think it's no big deal. But the words you use say a lot about who you are and what you believe.

Show that you respect girls and believe in gender equity by daring to not use any language that disrespects girls. And every time you hear something negative being said about a girl, counter it with two positive things or say "That's not cool."

DARE TO
USE SOCIAL MEDIA
FOR GOOD

SOCIAL MEDIA CAN BE A DOUBLE-EDGED SWORD. AT ITS BEST, IT allows us to connect with friends, to share things that are important to us, and to be a part of a global community. Some people have even used it to take important issues to the public. But at its worst, it's been used to spread rumors about people, to say mean and hurtful things, to troll, and to leave anonymous comments that people would never say in person.

If you're on social media, dare to use it for good. Talk to your followers about things that are important to you. Use it to cheer your friends on. If you're raising money for an organization or participating in an event that benefits a good cause, talk about it on social media. Dare to make your community better by raising awareness about important things in your feed.

DARE TO
THINK DIFFERENTLY
ABOUT GENDER

FROM THE MOMENT WE'RE BORN, WE'RE TOLD THAT CERTAIN things are for boys and certain things are for girls. That's why baby boys are often dressed in blue and baby girls in pink. Those made-up rules are called gender norms. But there's no real reason for these rules, and sometimes they keep us from being our authentic selves. Lots of boys take dance classes, and plenty of girls ride dirt bikes.

This week, dare to think differently about gender. Think about times when you were told "Boys don't do that," and make a list of the things you've felt pressured not to do. Is something holding you back from trying one of them? Now might be the time to finally get involved with one of them and make sure you aren't missing out on something you'd love!

DARE TO
ASK FOR CONSENT

HAS SOMEONE EVER COME UP BEHIND YOU AND YANKED YOUR hoodie? Or have they hugged you out of the blue when you weren't feeling it? Were you annoyed? You had a right to be. No matter what, everyone should ask for permission before coming into someone's personal space. That's what consent is all about—asking permission and getting a clear, definitive, enthusiastic yes before touching someone. Consent shows respect and makes sure everyone is cool with what's about to happen.

DARE TO
TALK ABOUT THE THING
THAT WORRIES YOU MOST

LIFE CAN BE SCARY BECAUSE IT DOESN'T COME WITH AN instruction manual. There's no right or wrong way to do lots of things, so sometimes we worry about how we'll react to the really scary stuff. Are you worried about your pet getting old and dying? Do you fear getting sick and ending up in the hospital? There are lots of situations that can grip someone's mind and not let go. Have you discussed with anyone the thing you worry about most? Usually, when we share our fears with a trusted person, those anxieties become less scary.

This week, dare to talk with a friend or parent about a very scary, very real fear. Explain what it is and why you feel that way. Share how the worry affects your life, and together you may be able to come up with some great ideas for defeating that fear's control over you.

DARE TO
CREATE A POSITIVE
PLAYLIST

SOMETIMES IT FEELS REALLY, REALLY GOOD TO PUT ON MUSIC while you're getting ready for school in the morning, walking down the sidewalk, or just letting loose in your room. Are there songs that make you want to get up and dance? Songs that make you feel great, that you can't help but sing or rap along to? Music has the power to help us tap into our feelings, whether it's making us even more energized when we're happy or pumping us up when we've been down.

This month, dare to create a positive playlist filled with songs that make you feel good about being you, that don't put anyone down, and that inspire you. Create a new playlist for each month, and by the end of the year you'll have twelve different playlists you can turn to, and a cool way to look back on the year.

DARE TO
BE SUPPORTIVE

HAVE YOU EVER MADE A CHOICE ABOUT WHAT TO WEAR, HOW TO cut your hair, or what to eat for lunch and someone close to you thought it was weird? Did their judgment surprise you and make you feel bad about your choice? At the end of the day, our personal choices usually affect only us, so it's strange that people get caught up in things that don't really concern them. Keep this in mind while being supportive of your friends' choices—as long as they're safe ones. Your support will allow them to be true to themselves without having a fear of judgment.

All month long, dare to be supportive of your friends' swag, what they want to do, and how they express themselves.

DARE TO
TRY A NEW
EXTRACURRICULAR
ACTIVITY

>>>———<<<

YOU'VE PROBABLY GOT YOUR SCHEDULE DOWN PRETTY TIGHT BY now. There's no doubt you have enough homework. Plus some hobbies and activities, too. Take a look around at what else your school and community have to offer. See a club or activity that interests you? If there's an opportunity to attend a meeting, try to go. You don't have to commit to something new if you're not into it or you're too busy. It never hurts to branch out and see what else exists.

This month, dare to join in on something. Seek out a hobby, sport, study group, or activity that you're interested in and try it out. If you can't find the perfect one, think about creating your own!

DARE TO
THINK ABOUT HOW
WOMEN ARE TREATED
IN VIDEO GAMES

WHEN YOU'VE PLAYED VIDEO GAMES, HAVE YOU NOTICED WHAT the female characters are like? No matter the setting, it seems that they're either damsels in distress waiting to be rescued, props on the sidelines, or not even available to choose as an avatar. Usually, they're also dressed in a way that makes you focus on their bodies instead of their kick-butt skills. There are even games that give you extra points for acting violently toward women. You wouldn't and shouldn't treat girls you know in real life this way, so why is it okay in a video game?

The next time you're playing video games with the guys, take a look at how women and girls are shown. Dare to stop playing video games that don't respect their female characters.

DARE TO
NOT INTERRUPT GIRLS

DID YOU KNOW THAT BOYS INTERRUPT GIRLS MUCH MORE THAN they interrupt boys? Living a healthy manhood means respecting girls' ideas just as much as boys' ideas and showing that respect by giving girls the time and space to say what they have to say.

This week, dare to not interrupt girls when they speak, and if another boy does, try to let him know *"She was speaking."* This is an easy way to be an ally and see things from a new perspective.

DARE TO
FIND A SHERO

DO YOU HAVE A HERO? WHAT ABOUT A *SHERO*? A SHERO IS A female version of a male hero. Just like her male counterparts, she shows strength under pressure and is an example of what's possible. She's inspiring and triumphant.

Dare to find a shero who impresses and motivates you. Write down what you admire about that person. Find a picture of her to keep on your phone, on your computer, in your locker, or in your room as a reminder of why she's your shero.

DARE TO
LEARN SOMETHING NEW
FROM A FRIEND

DO YOU EVER LOOK AROUND AT THE PEOPLE IN LINE AT THE STORE with you or fellow travelers at the airport or other moviegoers at the theater and wonder what their talents are? On any given day, we're surrounded by interesting and uniquely talented people. There's a good chance that even the people we know best have hidden talents.

This weekend, ask a friend to teach you something they're good at. It doesn't have to be flashy. Maybe they know how to juggle, level up on a video game, or curl their tongue in three different ways. You may be surprised to learn that your cousin can knit or your best friend can toss pizza dough (we love pizza around here). One thing we rely on from our friends is feeling seen and heard, because it makes us feel like we're accepted and not alone. When you ask a friend to share their talents with you, everyone wins: they feel good about themselves and you learn something new.

DARE TO
SEE A NEED—
AND MEET IT

WHEN YOU'RE WALKING DOWN THE HALL AT SCHOOL OR OUT running errands with your parents, look around and see how many people go through their day rushing from one thing to the next, often staring down at their phones. They're missing a lot that's happening right around them! There could be an elderly person struggling with their shopping bags, some snacks and trash left on the school bleachers, or a pet that seems lost. There are lots of opportunities for us to pitch in and help out in our communities.

Every day this week, dare to look around for things that could benefit from your help—and when you see a need, meet it!

DARE TO
REPLACE A BAD HABIT

IS THERE SOMETHING YOU DO REGULARLY THAT YOU'D LIKE TO change? Maybe you text too much during meals or can't put your phone down long enough to focus on what your friends are saying. Some people say "um" or "like" all the time. Others use swear words when they're frustrated.

Write down five habits that you'd like to break and dare to replace one with something positive. Maybe you'd like to stop chewing gum because you end up swallowing it, so you replace gum with mints. Pay attention to the times you successfully avoid your old habit, as well as the times you don't. But don't beat yourself up over that. It's simply meant to be a helpful tracker so you can keep doing that new, positive thing instead. Experts say that, on average, it takes twenty-one days of doing something to form a new habit, so don't give up!

DARE TO
TRY A NEW LOOK

HAVE YOU EVER BEEN IN A STORE AND THOUGHT, *DANG, THAT'S such a cool look, but I could never pull it off?* What stopped you from giving it a try? Was it because you thought you'd look out of place or that it wasn't made for someone like you? The clothes you choose help define your personal style, and it's okay to try new things! You may decide that look isn't for you after all, but at least you gave it a go and didn't make up your mind before seeing the outcome. Being true to yourself—embracing your authentic self—will keep you happier and healthier.

Next time you're out shopping, dare to try a new look and see how it feels.

DARE TO
DREAM WILD

IF YOU COULD ACHIEVE THREE OF YOUR LIFE'S BIGGEST DREAMS, what would they be? Do you want to write a book or visit a foreign country? Backpack through a mountain range or dive deep into the ocean? Discover a new animal or save an endangered one? Cure cancer? Travel beyond our galaxy and discover life on another planet? Do you have really big dreams that you've never told anyone because they seem too wild?

Maybe you really haven't spent much time thinking about your future, and that's okay, too. Now's the perfect time! Dare to test the limits of your dreams. This week, write down three dreams you have for yourself and think about what you can do to achieve them.

DARE TO SWITCH CHORES WITH THE GIRLS IN YOUR FAMILY

HAVE YOU NOTICED THAT YOU'RE ALWAYS ASKED TO TAKE OUT THE trash? If you have a sister, is she usually expected to do the dishes? There's no reason why chores should be divided up by gender. That reinforces stereotypes, including the ones that say girls should like being in the kitchen and boys should like mowing the lawn. Plenty of boys would rather be flipping pancakes, while lots of girls would love to be outside working in the yard.

Talk to your family about switching up the chores this week. Offer to do something around the house you wouldn't normally do or lend a hand on those really tough chores. Bonus: it'll get done twice as fast, leaving you double the amount of time to do more fun things.

DARE TO
OPEN A DOOR
FOR SOMEONE

SOMETIMES WE'RE IN SUCH A RUSH THAT WE FORGET HOW FAR A simple gesture can go. Holding a door open for someone to pass through is one of the best ways of saying *I see you, and I want to make your day easier.* For only a few seconds, you share a moment of kindness with whomever you help.

You can also open a door for someone by creating an opportunity for them. Nominate a classmate for special recognition at school, vote for your friend who's competing in a contest, or let someone else be the captain on your team if you're just playing something for fun. Throughout the year, dare to open doors for people.

DARE TO
TAKE CARE OF YOURSELF

SOMETIMES WE LOVE SO MANY THINGS IN LIFE THAT WE overcommit ourselves. You want to meet before school to study? Sure! Want to get lunch later? Absolutely. How about a game in the park? Done! Wanna catch a movie? And then go to the mall? And then play video games? Spending time with our friends while also balancing school and other commitments can be exhausting. It often leads to feeling burned out, which is a real bummer for your moods. One day you're feeling great and the next you're grouchy and exhausted and can't pay attention to what's going on around you.

This month, dare to take a step back, listen to your body, and learn how to take care of yourself. This can mean going to bed early one night, eating healthier foods, and politely saying no to things that maybe don't interest you and will take up too much of your time.

DARE TO
UNDERSTAND YOUR
OWN PRIVILEGE

HAVING PRIVILEGE MEANS THAT YOU WERE BORN WITH SOME sort of advantage that you didn't haven't to "earn." For example, because you are a boy, you have male (gender) privilege. If you're white, you have white (race) privilege. If your family has enough money for food, a place to live, and everything you need and want, you have financial privilege. Having privilege doesn't mean your life is easy. It simply means no one has questioned you or your ability because of your race, gender, or status.

Dare to look at your life and what you were born with and the circumstances you were raised in. Dare to understand your privilege and talk about how you can use it to help empower others who might not have the advantages you have.

DARE TO
FOCUS ON THE GOOD

DID YOU WAKE UP TIRED AND GET TO BREAKFAST ONLY TO FIND out someone had polished off the last bowl of your favorite cereal? On the way to school, did the bus driver tell you to hurry and you tripped and fell, so everyone laughed at you? It's tempting to let a few small frustrations ruin your day. But did someone in your family offer to get you something else for breakfast? Did someone ask if you were okay and help you up after you fell?

Instead of complaining about all the things that went wrong, dare to focus on the good things that came out of an unfortunate situation. No matter what happens around you, you are in control of how you respond. Don't waste a day because of a few minor setbacks!

DARE TO
OFFER A HUG

HUGS MAKE OUR BRAINS RELEASE CHEMICALS THAT CAUSE US TO feel happy and safe and take away pain and sadness. A simple hug can change someone's day for the better. Hugs show people that you care, that they're not alone, and that you want to understand what they're going through.

Dare to offer a hug when you think someone might need cheering up. Of course, don't forget to ask for consent before going for it!

DARE TO
CREATE SOMETHING

DO YOU HAVE A TOTALLY GENIUS IDEA TO INVENT SOMETHING brand-new? So many things out there exist because someone had an idea to create something—and then they put in the work to make it a reality! Once upon a time, things like rideshares, music streaming services, and *all* the apps on your phone didn't exist. Someone thought them up. Do you have an idea that you think is unique and amazing? It could be a school campaign, a new game, an app, or a way to help your community.

This month, dare to create something. Even if it's a work in progress, being creative is a way to celebrate our uniqueness and share something we care about. Not to mention, you could invent the next iPhone!

DARE TO
SET BOUNDARIES

HOW MANY TIMES HAS A RELATIVE YOU DON'T REMEMBER GONE IN for a hug you didn't expect? Have you ever let a classmate copy your homework because they'll get a failing grade and detention if they turn in a blank page? You never want to, but you feel like you should. Well, you shouldn't, my friend! Boundaries keep us healthy, safe, and out of trouble. If you don't want to sit in someone's lap or give them a hug or share a soda, you can politely say "No, thank you." And if your friend's asking you to bend the rules and you know it isn't right, you can just say "I'm sorry, I can't."

Dare to set three personal boundaries that make you feel comfortable. Talk to a parent about those boundaries and ask for their support.

DARE TO
GET INVOLVED WITH
A GOOD CAUSE

WHAT ISSUES ARE YOU PASSIONATE ABOUT? YOU MIGHT HAVE A family member who has overcome cancer or heart disease. Maybe you know someone who has trouble with reading or math. Is promoting equality important to you?

This month, dare to support an organization, cause, or group that's meaningful to you. Whether you support them through word of mouth by telling people all about their good work, through raising money, or through volunteering, the important thing is that you're getting involved. It's another great way of showing you're a compassionate person!

DARE TO
NOT JUDGE GIRLS

HAVE YOU EVER SEEN OR HEARD A GROUP OF BOYS TALKING about girls in a negative way? Were they making fun of the girls for what they were wearing or how they looked? Boys often "have fun" at the expense of girls. Sometimes grown men do this, too. It's not right when men or boys participate in this behavior. It's one of the many harmful teachings of the Man Box.

This week, dare to not judge girls—for their looks, their clothes, their abilities, or anything. Rather than making a judgment on a girl, go above and beyond by offering your encouragement to her!

DARE TO
SPEND TIME ALONE

WE SPEND SO MUCH OF OUR DAYS WITH AND AROUND OTHER people. Think about how many hours you spend at school, hanging out with friends and family, and all the time devoted to activities. When do you find time to just chill by yourself? Reading, thinking, daydreaming, and resting quietly can make you smarter, healthier, and more creative. Not only will you experience more "aha" moments, but you'll start connecting with your own feelings and learning more about yourself. It's important to spend time alone and learn how to like being alone—a skill that will benefit you for life!

This week, dare to set aside at least fifteen minutes each day just for you. You can do whatever you like— just roll solo and tech-free.

DARE TO
REMAIN ENDLESSLY
CURIOUS

HAVE YOU EVER BEEN AROUND A KID WAY YOUNGER THAN YOU who's constantly asking *Why? Why is the sky blue? Why does a dog bark? Why can't I eat the whole box of cereal for dinner?* Children are naturally curious because they're still learning about the big, wide world around them. But as kids get older, they usually stop asking so many questions. Maybe they don't want to look too interested in something. Maybe they don't know the answer and feel like everyone else does, so they're too embarrassed to ask. (Take it from us: You should ask! Someone will undoubtedly say "I didn't know that, either. I'm so glad you asked!") Or maybe they simply don't let their imagination run wild like they used to.

This week, dare to tap into your curiosity and ask *why*. Dare to open a book or newspaper and read something new. Dare to search for something on the internet you've always been curious about, like how to play the drums or what happened during a historical event you've heard mentioned. Never stop being curious, because it's how you learn, create, and find new things to love doing!

DARE TO
CALL OUT MAN BOX
BEHAVIOR

NOW THAT YOU KNOW ALL ABOUT MAN BOX BEHAVIOR, CONSIDER what you can do when you see it. We know groups of boys—friends, teammates, classmates, and neighbors—who have taken what they've learned and, together, decided to call out Man Box behavior. When someone tells inappropriate jokes or puts down a girl or a peer, these boys simply say (and now you can, too) "Man Box" as a positive way of holding each other accountable. Dare to talk about Man Box behavior and call it out when you see it.

GLOSSARY

The Book of Dares includes some words and phrases that we think are really important to get right. Just in case you're unfamiliar with any of them, we've included definitions here. You can find some of these in the dictionary, and some were created by A CALL TO MEN, based on our twenty-plus years of working with men and boys.

ASPIRING ALLY—someone who wants to support a person or group of people who don't always get treated fairly

AUTHENTIC SELF—one's whole, genuine, and real self

CISGENDER—when your gender identity (how you feel) matches the sex you were assigned at birth—for example, someone who identifies as a man and was also born male

COLLECTIVE SOCIALIZATION—how a group of people are taught to adapt to the norms or expectations of a culture or society

CONSENT—permission for you to do something or an agreement to do something

DIVERSITY—the idea that individuals are unique and should be valued for their differences (race, ethnicity, gender, sexual orientation, socioeconomic status, physical abilities, religious beliefs, political beliefs, or other ideologies)

ETHNICITY—cultural factors such as nationality, regional culture, ancestry, and language. Ethnicity is typically not immediately visible to others

GENDER EQUITY—the idea that all people should have the same rights, resources, opportunities, protections, and respect, no matter their gender

GENDER NORMS—the made-up roles and behaviors often associated with males and females, like the idea that girls wear pink and boys wear blue

HEALTHY MANHOOD—a way of living that allows men and boys to be their authentic selves. The principles of healthy manhood are: embracing and expressing a full range of emotion, not giving in to the pressure to always be fearless and in control, valuing and treating women, girls, and all people equally, never using language that puts people down, being interested in women and girls even if you don't romantically like them, and modeling healthy, respectful behavior for others.

MAN BOX—a phrase made up by A CALL TO MEN to show how men and boys are taught to view manhood. In the Man Box, men are supposed to be powerful, dominating, tough, successful, and fearless. In the Man Box, women and girls are seen as objects, as the property of men, and as having less value than men and boys. The teachings of the Man Box can be harmful to people of all genders.

NONBINARY AND/OR GENDER-NONCONFORMING—when your gender expression (behavior, appearance, mannerisms, interests) is different from typical expressions of masculinity or femininity. Nonbinary people sometimes use pronouns such as they, them, theirs.

PRIVILEGE—an advantage someone is born with that they didn't do anything to earn

RACE—a term used to describe people by their skin color, as well as other physical and biological traits. Race is typically visible to others.

SOCIALIZATION—how someone adapts their behavior to the norms or expectations of a culture or society

SOCIAL JUSTICE—the idea that everyone should enjoy equal rights and opportunities and not be treated unfairly

STEREOTYPE—a mistaken idea or belief many people have about a group of people or a thing

TRANSGENDER, OR TRANS—when your gender identity (how you feel) does not match the sex that you were assigned at birth—for example, someone who identifies as a female but was born male

UNCONSCIOUS BIAS—a thought or judgment about a person or situation that someone has because of background, race, gender, culture, religion, or personal experiences

UNDERREPRESENTED GROUP—a group of people who are less visible because of their race, gender ethnicity, or sexual orientation

LETTER TO FAMILY AND FRIENDS

Dear Family and Friends,

Thank you for supporting the boys in your life as they dare to feel confident about who they truly are and learn how to treat people around them with kindness and respect. Being a boy—being male—is a wonderful thing. We want to make every boy's lived experience the very best it can be. The dares in this book are meant to be fun and challenging and to help boys (and the adults in their lives) think and talk about different experiences that boys go through on their way to manhood. We believe that all kids will benefit from the dares in this book, but we have specifically and intentionally designed them to relate to the experience of boys and how they are often taught to view women and girls as inferior to men and boys.

HOW BOYS ARE TAUGHT TO BE MEN

A CALL TO MEN coined the term *Man Box* to illustrate
the collective socialization of men (how boys are taught
to view manhood and what society says it means to "be a
man"). There are so many good things about being a man—
more than we can mention! We want to look closely at the
teachings of the Man Box that can present problems for
boys as they grow up. Keep in mind that the teachings of
the Man Box are not exclusive to men and boys, but society has deemed it important for men and boys to adapt
to these particular expectations of manhood. For example, men and boys are expected to be strong, aggressive,
dominating, powerful, and athletic; to be providers, pro-
tectors, decision makers, and leaders. But there are so
many other things that boys and men can be and do that
aren't viewed by society as important or desirable. For example, a man or boy who is nurturing, sensitive, loving,
and compassionate can be ridiculed and even thought to
be "less of a man."

These teachings are reinforced in things we say all
the time: that "big boys don't cry," that a boy should "man
up," that he is "acting like a girl," and that he needs to
"be a man." Those messages tell boys it's not okay—not
safe, even—to show emotion or be afraid. Boys are consistently pushed beyond their feelings to aggression, and

THE MAN BOX

No pain   Powerful   Women are objects

    Strong   In charge   Protector

No fear   No feelings   Decision maker

   Aggressive   No emotions (except anger)

No weakness   Courageous   Dominating

Athletic   Women are property   Tough

MAN BOX RULES

Don't be vulnerable.   Don't be too loving.

Don't be too caring.   Don't act like a woman.

                   Don't ask for help.

Don't be too nice or too kind.   Act like a man.

Always be in control.   Don't be too committed.

Don't show emotions.   Don't show weakness.

that aggression is reflected back to them in video games, music, movies, and pornography.

We live in a culture where the Man Box dominates. It polices boys, demanding that they obey its rules and punishing them if they fall short. This socialization leaves boys vulnerable to depression, anxiety, suicide, high-risk behaviors like vaping and alcohol or drug use, putting themselves in physical danger, and violence toward themselves and others.

The Man Box teaches that boys shouldn't need to ask for help, that they should have everything under control or be able to figure everything out on their own. This can create a damaging cycle of harm. It can make boys feel insecure, ashamed, and lonely. Here's how it can play out:

Michael is having trouble with science class but doesn't ask for help because he doesn't want to look dumb (the Man Box says he should know it all!). Because he didn't ask for help, he fails an important test. Because he fails a test, he starts to doubt himself and thinks he's not smart. Because he's doubting himself, he quits trying in school. Michael has a bad semester and gets kicked off the basketball team because he didn't make his grades. Because he no longer has practice, he starts hanging out after school with kids who are making poor choices. Eventually, Michael starts making poor choices and gets in trouble with the police. He's suspended from school. His future is in real jeopardy.

We call this the cycle of consequences, and for many boys, it's very real.

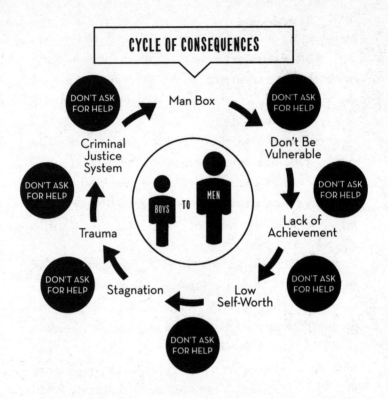

CYCLE OF CONSEQUENCES

DON'T ASK FOR HELP

Man Box

DON'T ASK FOR HELP

Criminal Justice System

Don't Be Vulnerable

DON'T ASK FOR HELP

DON'T ASK FOR HELP

BOYS TO MEN

Lack of Achievement

Trauma

DON'T ASK FOR HELP

DON'T ASK FOR HELP

Stagnation

Low Self-Worth

DON'T ASK FOR HELP

DON'T ASK FOR HELP

The Man Box also teaches boys to view women, girls, and those who are LGBQ, trans, and gender nonconforming as having less value than men. Boys start getting these "less than" messages in their early, formative years. On the ball field, a coach might say to a boy, "Son, you've got to throw harder than that, you throw like a ___." Most men and boys around the world fill in that blank with *girl* (that's our collective socialization!). So what does that boy walk away thinking about girls? That they're weak and inferior—and that you certainly don't want to be like one. The coach isn't trying to teach the kid about girls. He just wants the boy to throw harder. But the lesson that coach passes along creates the fertile soil where sexism can take root.

Similarly, boys who are physically weak or who present more "feminine" qualities or behaviors are demeaned with gender-based insults. Boys who push the norms of gender expression with colored hair, painted nails, and other personal style choices consistently have their manhood questioned. All those who fall outside the Man Box are at risk of isolation, bullying, and violence.

THE SOLUTION: HEALTHY MANHOOD

Healthy manhood is the solution. It's the antidote for some of the most destructive problems we face in our society—bullying, dating violence, domestic violence, sexual harassment, sexual assault, mass shootings, male suicide, gender-based discrimination, and homophobia. The threat of all these problems decreases as we increase healthy manhood.

Healthy manhood is also linked to improved physical health and emotional well-being for men. When boys are told not to cry or feel, there are lasting negative effects on their health and relationships. The Man Box teaches boys to stuff their feelings inside or only act them out in a physical or aggressive manner. Aggression is a very good thing if boys are playing a sport or competing in a race. But aggression toward friends, family, and even themselves can be harmful. We must help boys develop the skills to identify their feelings and the language to express them. Boys' emotional literacy is directly linked to their potential for happiness and success.

This book will, we hope, help boys see the ways they are taught to be men, and how some of those teachings can keep boys from becoming their whole, authentic selves. The dares promote healthy manhood and authenticity, help develop leadership skills, and encourage gender equity—all of which can help create a world where all men and boys are loving and respectful and all women and girls are valued and safe.

The dares in this book are based on A CALL TO MEN's more than twenty years of experience working with and training men and boys, including the National Football League, the National Basketball Association, Major League Baseball, Major League Soccer, the National Hockey League, the United States military, the US Department of Justice, the United Nations, corporations, educational institutions, and other organizations across the United States and abroad.

Finally, *The Book of Dares* was written with mad love for boys and men, with a profound respect for humanity, and with deep gratitude for the honor of supporting the evolution of manhood.

Ted Bunch and Anna Marie Johnson Teague
A CALL TO MEN

ACKNOWLEDGMENTS

We are incredibly grateful to the powerful visionaries who have supported the work of A CALL TO MEN from the very beginning. We would not be shaping the next generation of manhood without your love, support, and guidance.

To our funders and partners: Your investment in our work planted the seed for lasting social change. We remain devoted to nurturing this global community of men, boys, and allies committed to ending all forms of gender-based violence and discrimination.

We offer our humble and heartfelt thanks to our editor, Sara Sargent, for bravely championing this project and lovingly guiding us through the process. You are forever part of the A CALL TO MEN family.

There will never be enough thank-yous for our brilliant CEO, Tony Porter, or for the leadership team, staff, and board of A CALL TO MEN. We are incredibly blessed to be in this work together.

FROM TED BUNCH

I want to thank Michelle Kydd Lee and Cait Hoyt at CAA for their belief in me and in the importance of promoting healthy manhood. I also want to express my deep gratitude to my incredible writing partner, Anna Marie Johnson Teague, for her brilliance and selflessness, and to my cofounding partner and friend, Tony Porter.

I joyfully acknowledge and embrace my amazing family, who nurture, inspire, and bless me every day. Thank you, Desiree, Kimm, Maya, Josh, Jalen, Kachikwu, Erica, and Matt, for your never-ending love and support.

Finally, all praise is to God for my life and for allowing me to spend each day with people I love as we work to create a world where all men and boys are loving and respectful and all women, girls, LGBQ, trans, and gender-nonconforming people are valued and safe.

FROM ANNA MARIE JOHNSON TEAGUE

To my buddy and collaborator, Ted Bunch: Your belief in me opened a door at A CALL TO MEN and allowed me to join this most gifted, dedicated, and inspirational team. I am so grateful to be learning from y'all.

To my mom and dad, for working so hard to give me every possible opportunity and for cheering me on every step of the way. Any accomplishments I may have are built on the foundation that you gave to me. To my sister, Elizabeth—you are beautiful and can do the hard things. I believe in you. To my brother, Garner—you were my first baby. Our relationship taught me how to love being a boy mom.

To my boys—Chad and Jack—thanks for loving ALL of me. Especially the parts that are inconvenient and don't always fit in. Chad, you bless me and Jack in a thousand ways. You are a devoted husband, father, and son, and you've been working out your version of healthy manhood since I met you in the seventh grade. Jack, you are the reason I do this work—so that you can be you. Hold tight to your goodness and your joy. And know that God is so faithful.